Hello!
I am your New Teacher

Written by Jahleia Box
Illustrated by Sasha Beytler

Dedicated to Elizabeth and Madison.

Hello and welcome students; I am your new teacher!
If you know my name already, well that is just fine!
I will know your names and faces too in just no time!

You have said goodbye to summer and your parents, and that was a very hard thing to do! In no time, we will be family, learn so much, and have fun while doing it too!

Today will be an easy day, so try your best to relax!

Now, find your desk and chair, the one with your name tags attached!

I know your backpacks are bursting with the cool supplies that your parents bought for you!

I will show you where to unload them and exactly what to do!

In place of those folders, sharpeners, crayons, and sticks of glue,
I will give you some very important papers that must be signed by your parents and some by you!

Speaking of important papers, the paper that your parents cannot disregard!

The paper that tells us who to contact if you get sick or hurt, and it is called your "Emergency Contact Card!"

Now, let's get down to business and not waste any more time.

I am going to share with you my expectations of how to form a line.

The job of a line leader is a very responsible task.

The line leader shows what to do in line, so you will not have to ask.

Well, what happens this time if you are not chosen? Is that a reason to pout?

Of course not, we have the entire school year to figure things out!

Another class job that is just as special and calls for order!

Is the amazing job of door holder!

The door holder is polite and makes sure everyone leaves safe!

When they have completed their job, they return quietly back to their place!

Soon it'll be time to eat, so grab your ham and cheese sandwiches, with sliced cucumbers.

If you did not bring your lunch, there's no need to worry, I have your lunch numbers.

Once you have your special lunch number, in the line you will go through!

The cafeteria lady will smile and say, "Next!" as she waves at you!

At some point in our day, we will meet teachers that teach Art, Music, Spanish, and PE.

Treat them with respect, the same way you would treat me.

They are your special teachers, and they show you how to create.

Therefore, we must get to their class on time and try not to be late!

The day will come soon where you will have to take some placement tests.

These tests tell me what you need to learn, so you must try your absolute best.

After you take these tests, I will talk to you and keep you in the loop!

I will use the results to put you in your brand-new group!

In your cool new group, you will learn with your friends, and you will come and see me too.

Every day will be a set of directions that will show you just what to do!

Your parents will have plenty of questions for me, I know this without a doubt.

I get to answer all their great questions soon at the open house!

So, as you can see, we have so many wonderful things that we are going to learn and do!

I am your new teacher for the year; take my hand and I promise with love and care, I will guide you through!

www.ingramcontent.com/pod-product-compliance
Lightning Source LLC
LaVergne TN
LVHW071108160826
845679LV00004B/1012

* 9 7 9 8 8 4 4 0 9 3 9 0 6 *